EXPLORING CIVIL RIGHTS

THE RISE

1970

SELENE CASTROVILLA

Franklin Watts®

An imprint of Scholastic Inc

T0002421

Content Consultant

A special thank you to Ryan M. Jones at the
National Civil Rights Museum for his expert consultation.

Library of Congress Cataloging-in-Publication Data
Names: Castrovilla, Selene, 1966– author.
Title: The rise: 1970 / Selene Castrovilla.
Other titles: Exploring civil rights.
Description: First edition. | New York : Franklin Watts, an imprint of
   Scholastic Inc., 2023. | Series: Exploring civil rights | Includes
   bibliographical references and index. | Audience: Ages 10–14. |
   Audience: Grades 7–9. | Summary: "Series continuation. Narrative
   nonfiction, key events of the Civil Rights Movement in the years after
   1965. Photographs throughout"—Provided by publisher.
Identifiers: LCCN 2022039913 (print) | LCCN 2022039914 (ebook) |
   ISBN 9781338837599 (library binding) | ISBN 9781338837605 (paperback) |
   ISBN 9781338837612 (ebk)
Subjects: LCSH: African Americans—Civil rights—History—20th
   century—Juvenile literature. | Civil rights movements—United
   States—History—20th century—Juvenile literature. | Civil rights
   workers—United States—Juvenile literature. | BISAC: JUVENILE
   NONFICTION / Social Topics / Civil & Human Rights | JUVENILE NONFICTION
   / History / General
Classification: LCC E185.615 .C356 2023 (print) | LCC E185.615 (ebook) |
   DDC 323.1196/073—dc23/eng/20220823
LC record available at https://lccn.loc.gov/2022039913
LC ebook record available at https://lccn.loc.gov/2022039914

10 9 8 7 6 5 4 3 2 1   23 24 25 26 27

Printed in China   62
First edition, 2023

Composition by Kay Petronio

COVER & TITLE PAGE: Michigan State University's incoming president Dr. Clifton Wharton, Jr., and his wife wave to the crowd at a football game.

Congresswoman Shirley Chisholm and her all-female staff, page 37.

Table of Contents

Edwin Starr, page 54.

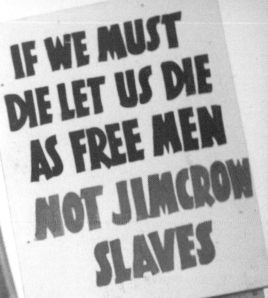

IF WE MUST DIE LET US DIE AS FREE MEN NOT JIMCROW SLAVES

An African American man demands the end of Jim Crow laws at a 1960s civil rights protest.

The Way It Was

The year 1865 was an important one in U.S. history. The American Civil War (1861–1865) ended and the Thirteenth **Amendment** to the U.S. Constitution was passed, **abolishing** slavery. This period of time also introduced Black codes in the form of **Jim Crow** laws. These laws restricted where people of color could live and work and were especially strict in the American South.

Jim Crow laws enforced **segregation**. Under the racial policy of "separate but equal," Black Americans could be given access to separate facilities if their quality was equal to that of white facilities. In reality, however, there was no equality. African Americans were forced to attend separate and inadequate schools and live in run-down neighborhoods.

The Fight Begins

As Jim Crow practices continued, two prominent **civil rights** organizations emerged. The National Association of Colored Women's Clubs (NACWC) was founded in 1896 by a group of politically active women, including Harriet Tubman. Members of the association dedicated themselves to fighting for voting rights and for ending racial violence in the form of **lynchings** against African Americans.

The National Association for the Advancement of Colored People (NAACP), founded in 1909, followed in the NACWC's footsteps. The NAACP focused on opposing segregation and Jim Crow policies. Both organizations would be crucial in the coming fight for justice.

Lasting Changes

In the following years, the Great Depression (1929–1939) and World War II (1939–1945) left Black Americans fighting for their lives at home and overseas. The 1954 U.S. Supreme Court decision in the *Brown v. Board of Education of Topeka* case challenging school segregation finally put an end to "separate but equal" in public schools. The years between 1955 and 1965 would serve as the heart of the civil rights movement. Rosa Parks refused to give up her seat on a bus, sparking the Montgomery bus **boycott**. The Reverend Dr. Martin Luther King, Jr., emerged as a leader and organized the March on Washington for Jobs and Freedom, the largest civil rights demonstration at the time.

The 1960s and 1970s further ignited those yearning for equal opportunities under the law. **Activists** continued to persevere, resulting in lasting changes for the African American community.

Civil rights activist Fannie Lou Hamer worked for Black voting rights and women's rights in 1970.

1970

In this book, read about the state of American civil rights in 1970 and learn about the divide between civil rights groups over how to proceed in the new decade. The greatest threat to obtaining civil rights had become the U.S. government. President Richard Nixon's administration was attempting to silence civil rights seekers by prosecuting them for crimes they did not commit. Civil rights leaders feared that no person of color could receive fair treatment in an American courtroom. The United States had waged war in Vietnam for five years, and thousands of young American men had been killed. With the nation exploding in protests, civil rights leaders were torn over whether the unjust war was a topic for them to address. The year would also see women rising up for their equal rights. Women of color would speak out about their experiences—and the mistreatment of one Black woman by the criminal justice system would ignite a movement of its own. ▪

From left to right: Elbert "Big Man" Howard, Donald "DC" Cox, and June Hilliard, three leaders of the Black Panther Party.

1

A Divided Movement

The new decade opened with a divided approach to obtaining civil rights for African Americans. The civil rights movement had focused on **integration** and working toward mutual equality. But the newer Black Power movement endorsed self-sufficiency for Black Americans. The two ideologies disagreed over the methods to achieve their goals: nonviolence versus "any means necessary."

Those supporting peaceful protests were still reeling from the assassination of Dr. Martin Luther King, Jr., on April 4, 1968. As head of the Southern Christian Leadership Conference (SCLC), King was the most influential and highly regarded member of the late 1950s and 1960s civil rights movement. His close friend and fellow activist Reverend Ralph Abernathy became SCLC's second president.

Although he tried, it was impossible for Abernathy to replicate the energy and creativity King had projected. The group was losing members—and the movement was losing momentum.

In contrast, Black Power was surging. The most prominent Black Power organization, the Black Panther Party for Self Defense, or Black Panthers, engaged in armed resistance against **white supremacists**. They were involved in many gunfire exchanges with the police—some fatal on both sides. Black Panther Party membership reached a peak in 1970, with offices in 68 cities and thousands of members.

The Panther 21

On the evening of January 14, 1970, famed conductor Leonard Bernstein and his wife, Felicia Montealegre, hosted a fundraiser for the "Panther 21." This was a group of 21 Black Panthers who had been charged with conspiracy to murder and bomb several places in New York City.

Donald Cox (right) with Leonard Bernstein and Felicia Montealegre's at the Panther 21 fundraiser.

A Man of Firsts

In January 1970, Dr. Clifton Wharton, Jr., began his term as Michigan State University's 14th president, becoming the first African American president of a major U.S. university.

This appointment was one of many firsts for Clifton, who has been called a "quiet pioneer." After graduating from Harvard University, where he entered at age 16, Wharton became the first African American to earn a master of arts degree in international affairs from Johns Hopkins University. Following this achievement, Wharton earned a master of arts and a PhD in **economics** from the University of Chicago.

Dr. Wharton served as Michigan State's president for eight years. In 1978, he became the first African American to head the State University of New York's 64-campus system—the nation's largest. And in 1987, he became the first Black chair and CEO of a major U.S. corporation, TIAA-CREF.

Dr. Clifton Wharton, Jr., was heralded for his contributions to Michigan State University during his eight years as its president.

FBI director
J. Edgar Hoover.

They had been jailed since April 2, 1969. The Panther 21 had no trial in all those months. They had no money to pay for a lawyer or their bail, which had been set much higher than the usual amount for such charges.

FBI director J. Edgar Hoover called the Black Panther Party "the greatest threat to the internal security of the country." But people who supported the rights and individual freedoms of American citizens felt that the Black Panthers were unjustly targeted by the government. The arrest of the Panther 21 appeared to be a case of the government overstepping its rights and trampling the rights of others. Some people believed the government's holding of the Panther 21 was politically motivated, **racist**, and lacking evidence. The Panther 21 were not receiving the fair treatment they were legally entitled to by the law.

The Bernsteins were among a group of New Yorkers who felt that the Panther 21 were being held unjustly. This group established a fund to help with legal expenses and to assist the families of the accused while the prisoners awaited trial. The gathering at the Bernstein apartment was held to raise awareness for the fund and gain contributions.

The party and its 90 attendees—many of them celebrities—would become harshly criticized by people who felt that the civil rights movement and all that Dr. King had worked for was being destroyed by the Black Power movement.

Instead of reporting on the issue of the Panther 21's violated rights in the news section, the *New York Times* featured a story about the event on its society page, a part of the newspaper that gossiped about fashionable events thrown and attended by the wealthy. Two days later, an article in the *New York Times* condemned the Panthers, the Bernsteins, and all their guests for undermining the serious efforts of those working for civil rights. The article stated that the party insulted the memory of King.

A button in support of the Panther 21.

The '60s Split

The divide in civil rights ideology had risen in the 1960s between two civil rights leaders: Dr. King and Malcolm X.

Malcolm X was a Black Nationalist. He believed African Americans should develop their own national identity, proudly separating from anyone else. In fact,

Dr. King (left) and Malcolm X meet at a 1964 Senate debate over the Civil Rights Act.

he felt that Black people should distance themselves in every way from white people and support themselves economically. He believed that any means were justified in achieving these goals, including violence. Malcolm X criticized anyone who cooperated with white people and fought for integration—especially King. Malcolm X called for a revolution of African American independence from white Americans. He said Black Americans could not simply say they would overcome racism and **discrimination**. They had to fight to overcome them.

On the contrary, King insisted that violence was not the answer. He had always preached and engaged in **nonviolent resistance**. King called nonviolent protest the refusal to cooperate with an evil system.

He believed this method, created by India's Mahatma Gandhi, "was one of the most potent weapons available to oppressed people in their struggle for freedom." Nonviolent methods of protest included rallies, demonstrations, boycotts, symbolic acts, and public speeches. King was conflicted when Malcolm X's ideology took a broad hold. He mourned the loss of hope in African Americans who embraced violence as a means to their end, and he recommitted to his belief in nonviolence.

Things grew more heated between the two men and between their supporters in 1964. The Mississippi Freedom Democratic Party, which was started to give Mississippi's African Americans a voice in government, was not permitted represen- tation at the 1964 Democratic National Convention,

Malcolm X insisted that African American civil rights should be achieved using any means necessary.

On August 28, 1963, Dr. King (center) and a group of civil rights activists lead the March on Washington.

despite winning that right in the state elections. Support grew for Malcolm X as more African Americans believed that white people would never accept Black people as equals.

Malcolm X was assassinated in 1965, and although his killers were members of the **Nation of Islam**, the group he had broken away from a year earlier and criticized, many African Americans believed the U.S. government was involved in his murder. Malcolm X's new organization, the Organization of Afro-American Unity (OAAU), had been called a threat to the national security of the United States by Hoover.

Alice Walker

Author and poet Alice Walker's first novel, *The Third Life of Grange Copeland*, was published in 1970 when Walker was 26.

Twelve years later, her most famous novel was published. *The Color Purple* won the Pulitzer Prize for Fiction, and Walker was the first Black woman to receive this award. The novel also won the National Book Award. It was made into an Academy Award–nominated movie starring Oprah Winfrey.

Walker's work examines racism and imperfect relationships among Black families. It has been both praised and criticized for its raw honesty.

Alice Walker was inspired to become a civil rights activist when she met Dr. King in the 1960s.

King called Malcolm X's death a great tragedy and said that the world had been deprived of a potentially great leader. King believed that Malcolm X had been coming to a better understanding of nonviolence. Just weeks earlier, Malcolm X had journeyed to Selma, Alabama, where King was imprisoned for leading a peaceful voter registration demonstration without a permit. He wanted to help King achieve his goals.

Malcolm X's murder sparked outrage in African American communities, and the push for Black **liberation** escalated.

Black Power Movement

Stokely Carmichael (who later became Kwame Ture) was the Student Nonviolent Coordinating Committee (SNCC) spokesperson and chair. SNCC had been formed by African American students in 1960, and it had been a leading force in nonviolent protest. But the group's dynamic had shifted following the 1964 Democratic

Stokely Carmichael delivers a speech calling for Black Power to students at the University of California, Berkeley.

National Convention. Most of SNCC's staff felt that the nonviolent approach to confronting hate was not working. On June 16, 1966, its position was firmly changed when Carmichael used the term "Black Power" as a political slogan.

The Black Power movement's clenched fist is a symbol of unity and resistance.

To Carmichael, the idea of Black Power was to bring individuals together within the movement. SNCC rejected **desegregation** as its primary objective. Its goal was to be separate and self-sufficient. It ejected its white members, and the Congress of Racial Equality (CORE) did the same. Soon, the *N* in SNCC would be changed from "Nonviolent" to "National."

Dr. King was critical of the growing Black Power movement. He said its weakness was its failure to see that the Black man and the white man needed each other.

The Black Panther Party considered themselves at war with the white supremacist power structure— but not with all white people. Bobby Seale, chair and cofounder of the Panthers, said that the oppression of Black people was mainly a result of economic **exploitation**. Seale said that working-class people of all colors needed to unite against the ruling class that exploited and oppressed them.

Educating Black Youth

The second Black Panther liberation school opened in Mount Vernon, New York, on July 17, 1970. The first one was founded in Richmond, Virginia, the year before.

The organization had decided to take the education of Black youth into their own hands after the Civil Rights Acts of 1964 and 1968 failed to equalize the quality of learning between Black children and white children. The Black Panthers felt that Black children were not being prepared for adulthood in public schools.

In addition to basic school curriculum, students were taught about Black history and culture. They were also made aware of class structure and racism and were instilled with the conviction to object to society's obstacles rather than accept them.

Students attend a Black Panther school called the Children's House in Oakland, CA.

Protests and Confusion

The fury over the Bernsteins' fundraiser grew, but its intentions were ignored. Felicia Montealegre Bernstein had been a member of the American Civil Liberties Union (ACLU) for years. This nonprofit organization had been founded in 1920 with the mission "to defend and preserve the individual rights and liberties guaranteed to every person in this country by the Constitution and laws of the United States."

Mrs. Bernstein wrote a letter to the *New York Times* that was published on January 21, 1970. Responding to the scathing editorial written about her and her husband, she criticized the *Times* for mocking a serious event that was focused on the civil liberties of the people awaiting trial. By reporting on the gathering as a "fashionable" event,

Like the Panther 21, Black Panther leader Bobby Seale was jailed on questionable charges.

Leonard Bernstein and Felicia Montealegre continued to be criticized for their support of the Panther 21.

the newspaper had lost its integrity and insulted everyone at the event.

Despite this letter, the Bernsteins were continually targeted for their support of the jailed Panthers. On June 8, 1970, an essay called "Radical Chic" by journalist and author Tom Wolfe appeared in *New York Magazine*. Once again, the Bernsteins were mocked. This essay was later reprinted in two of Wolfe's books. This continued uproar demonstrated the divided activism in the beginning of the 1970s. It was a split made even larger by the Vietnam War. ▪

The June 8, 1970, cover of *New York Magazine* mocked the Bernsteins.

Chicago Seven member Abbie Hoffman is arrested for trying to interrupt a Congressional hearing.

2

The Whole World Was Watching

The trial of the Chicago Seven went to the jury for **deliberations** on February 14, 1970.

David Dellinger, Rennie Davis, Tom Hayden, Abbie Hoffman, Jerry Rubin, Lee Weiner, and John Froines were all charged with crossing state lines into Chicago, Illinois, with the intention of starting a riot. They had originally been the Chicago Eight, also called the **Conspiracy** Eight. Bobby Seale was charged as well, but during the trial his case was separated out.

The charges rose from a riot outside the Democratic National Convention in Chicago between police and protesters on August 28, 1968.

These men had all been targeted by the FBI and President Nixon's administration as threats because they had spoken out against unjust

A massive police presence is seen at the Democratic National Convention.

government policies surrounding the war in Vietnam and police brutality. It was clear that the charges were not true—some of these men had never met before the convention, so how could they plan a riot together? Bobby Seale had not even been a scheduled speaker—he was a last-minute replacement.

The previous presidential administration had declined to press charges. But when Nixon took office in 1969, he and Hoover decided to have the eight men arrested and tried as an attempt to silence the peace movement against the war in Vietnam—and also the Black Power movement. The administration considered both movements threats because they were so vocal in their criticisms and rallied people to protest. The charges were justified through an anti-riot act added into the 1968 Civil Rights Act.

Defenseless

The police had started the riot, and the general public knew it. The protesters had been marching toward the convention when they met a blockade of police wearing riot helmets. Knowing they were in trouble, the protesters lay down in the street, chanting "the whole world is watching." The police attacked the protesters with clubs and Mace. For 17 minutes, Americans watched the brutal chaos on TV. Protesters were beaten and even shoved through storefront windows before being arrested.

Questioning Democracy

This case tested Americans' constitutional rights of freedom of speech and the freedom to assemble, or gather. It also became about the right of Americans to defend them-selves against criminal charges, and the fairness of the U.S. judi-cial system.

Judge Julius Hoffman denied the Chicago Eight their constitutional rights to a fair trial.

Seizing the Time

After Bobby Seale was granted his mistrial in Chicago, he was sent to a San Francisco jail to serve his four-year **contempt** sentence. Between November 1969 and March 1970, he told Arthur Goldberg, a reporter for the *San Francisco Bay Guardian*, the story of how he and Huey P. Newton met, created, and grew the Black Panther Party. Goldberg recorded the sessions, which were combined to become Seale's book *Seize the Time: The Story of the Black Panther Movement and Huey P. Newton*. Published in 1970, this book was immediately embraced by supporters of the Black Power movement, and it remains a "must read" of Black Power literature.

The cover of *Seize the Time* features a courtroom artist's sketch of Bobby Seale chained and gagged.

It questioned whether the police would be held responsible for their actions and whether victims could be legally blamed.

Presumed Guilty

From the start, the trial was anything but fair to the **defendants**. The judge, Julius Hoffman, made it clear he felt they were guilty. His mistreatment of the defendants escalated, and when they protested, he held them in contempt of court. This meant that they were charged with the crime of disrupting and/or disrespecting the proceedings and the judge. Respected civil rights attorney William Kunstler, one of the defendants' lawyers, was also charged with contempt.

Bobby Seale's contempt charges outnumbered everyone else's. He loudly refused to accept the injustice being done to him. The lawyer representing Seale was in the hospital, but Hoffman refused to delay the trial or allow Seale to act as his own attorney. Determined to silence Seale's protests, Hoffman ordered Seale to be chained and gagged in the courtroom. Seale remained that way for several days before finally receiving a mistrial—and a four-year prison sentence for 16 counts of contempt of court.

Judge Hoffman charged the remaining defendants and their lawyers with a total of 159 counts of

Silenced in court, the Chicago Seven hold a press conference during their trial to tell their side of the story.

criminal contempt. The sentences ranged from 2 months and 18 days to 48 months and 13 days.

Torn over Peace

In the previous decade, civil rights leaders had become harshly divided over whether to merge with the peace movement, which demanded the ending of the unjust Vietnam War. The United States had been involved in the war since 1954.

Organized opposition to U.S. involvement in Vietnam began in 1964, as President Lyndon B. Johnson began increasing the number of young American men being sent to the war.

In 1965, Johnson increased the number of young men **drafted** from 17,000 to 35,000 per month.

African American Think Tank

The Joint Center for Political and Economic Studies was founded in 1970 to help newly elected African American officials become powerful in the political field. It is a think tank, a place where a group of people gather to analyze, discuss, read, and write about important issues. The Joint Center not only trained Black elected officials in how to be effective, it also examined American policies as they related to people of color.

Louis E. Martin, a Chicago journalist, Black newspaper publisher, and civil rights activist, was a principal founder of the Joint Center, and he served as first chair of its board. He had been an adviser to two presidents: John F. Kennedy and Lyndon B. Johnson. Later, he would work with President Jimmy Carter.

The Joint Center became a haven for African American politicians such as Shirley Chisholm, the first Black woman elected to Congress. It continues to be a vital American think tank.

Louis E. Martin (left) meets with foreign leaders alongside Lyndon B. Johnson (right) as the president's adviser.

The November 1965 draft call was the largest since the Korean War.

The NAACP issued a statement against merging the civil rights and peace movements, while Dr. King laid out four powerful reasons why the civil rights movement did connect with the peace movement:

First, funds for poverty-stricken neighborhoods were cut to fund the war. Second, young Black men were dying in combat at much higher rates than young white men. Third, ignoring the violence of the war could be seen as accepting the use of violence to obtain social change. And finally, King's SCLC bore the motto "To save the soul of America." Surely, America's soul was being poisoned by immorally sending its young men to die in Vietnam for no good reason.

The Verdict

The jury returned on February 18, **acquitting** all the Chicago Seven of the conspiracy charge. Froines and Weiner were acquitted of all charges. However, Davis, Dellinger, Hayden, Hoffman, and Rubin were all found guilty of traveling between states with the intention of starting a riot.

Two days later, the defendants were finally allowed to speak when they made their statements before sentencing. David Dellinger said that no matter what happened to him and his codefendants, and however unjust that was, it would be little compared to what had already happened to Black people in the United States. Sending him and his codefendants to prison, he said, would not solve the country's rampant racism or its economic injustice.

Tom Hayden stated that he and his codefendants had been chosen as scapegoats by the government for all that the government wanted to prevent happening in the 1970s.

Judge Hoffman sentenced each of the men to five years in prison—the most he was allowed to impose. In addition, he fined them $5,000 each.

On February 28, the men were released on bail to await their appeal, where a new judge would hear arguments from both the defense and prosecution, study the evidence, and review the trial proceedings to see if the verdicts were justified. ■

The National Organization for Women (NOW) organized the Women's Strike for Equality.

3

Women Catch a Second Wave

American women won the right to vote in 1920, when the Nineteenth Amendment to the Constitution was ratified. The National Women's Party (NWP) was a political group that had ignited the fight for women's **suffrage**, riding a continuously mounting **feminist** wave. Women all over the country hopped on the swelling surf, riding it to victory. In 1921, the party announced its plans to work for an Equal Rights Amendment (ERA), which would allow Congress to enforce legal equality between men and women. The ERA was written by Alice Paul, leader of the NWP, and Crystal Eastman in 1923.

Fifty years after the Nineteenth Amendment was ratified, feminists were finally riding a second wave toward the Equal Rights Amendment. The women's liberation movement was surging—all thanks to the civil rights movement.

Witnessing the powerful results of the 1960s movement for Black equal rights, women realized that they, too, could organize and work together toward the equality they could not achieve individually.

Homemakers

Women were not allowed to get a credit card in the 1960s. They could not serve on federal juries or get an education at an Ivy League college even if they had the grades to get in. If they happened to obtain an office job, they were not paid as much as men, and they were often disrespected. These were just some of the inequities women faced. And even though discrimination in the workplace was outlawed by the Civil Rights Act

Female flight attendants in the 1960s were given age, height, and weight restrictions.

When Shirley Chisholm (center with glasses) became the first Black woman elected to Congress, she hired an all-female staff.

of 1964, the law was not enforced, and the injustices continued.

Equality N.O.W.

Admiring the success of the NAACP in establishing and advocating rights for African Americans, 28 women decided to start a similar organization for women in 1966. One of the women was Shirley Chisholm, a Black woman who was a member of the New York State Assembly. Chisholm often said she faced greater discrimination in her political pursuits as a woman than as a person of color. The organization was named the National Organization for Women (NOW).

Sisterhood Is Powerful

Sisterhood Is Powerful: An Anthology of Writings from the Women's Liberation Movement, a collection of feminist writings edited by Robin Morgan, was released in 1970.

Morgan was an early feminist and poet. As both an educational book designed to raise awareness and a call to action, this volume was credited with helping to fire up the women's liberation movement. The New York Public Library named it "One of the 100 most influential books of the 20th century."

Eleanor Holmes Norton, an African American lawyer who headed the New York City Human Rights Commission and held the nation's first hearings on discrimination against women, was one of the contributors to the book.

Robin Morgan speaks with a police officer during a feminist protest outside the Miss America Pageant.

Inspirational

The women of the civil rights movement were also inspiring to feminists. "What I saw was a different model of what it meant to be a woman," said Jo Freeman, a second wave feminist. Fannie Lou Hamer was one of these women.

Jo Freeman speaks at a meeting about women's liberation.

Born into a Mississippi farming family, Hamer witnessed racism from an early age. When some of their livestock was poisoned, Hamer

Fannie Lou Hamer (center) at a rally for the Mississippi Freedom Democratic Party.

said she knew a local white racist had done it because her family was successful. Determined to keep going, Hamer became a community organizer, fighting for Black voting rights. She started the Mississippi Freedom Democratic Party and organized Mississippi's Freedom Summer campaign for voter registration. After the triumph of the Freedom Democratic Party, she traveled to the 1964 Democratic National Convention as a delegate.

Holding Women Back

Hamer was one of the many Black women in the civil rights movement who were upset by the way men in the organization treated them. The men took credit for the ideas the women had, keeping the women out of the spotlight. Roy Wilkins, leader of the NAACP, told Hamer and other female activists at the 1964 Democratic National Convention that they were "ignorant of the political process, should listen to their leaders and just return home."

Ella Baker, who established and headed SNCC, was another inspiring female activist who was met with sexism. In 1970, Baker reflected that if she had not been a woman, she would have been well-known in certain places, and perhaps held certain kinds of positions. She was kept behind the scenes because of her gender.

The Jackson 5

1970 was a breakout year for the singing group the Jackson 5—brothers Jackie, Tito, Jermain Marlon, and Michael. "I Want You Back" was the band's first national single and became their first number-one hit on January 31.

In February, the group performed their song "ABC" on the TV show *American Bandstand*, where the brothers also each received an award for breakthrough sales. The next month, "ABC" became a number-one hit.

They held their first concert as Motown artists at the Philadelphia Civic Center on May 2, the start of their first tour. They also appeared on their first newspaper cover for *Soul*. Also in May, "The Love You Save" hit number one. And in October, "I'll Be There" became their fourth consecutive number-one song. They were the first group to achieve this feat.

Pictured left to right are Jermaine, Tito, Michael, Marlon, and Jackie Jackson in 1970.

Activist Ella Baker (left) and actress Ruby Dee at a news conference to protest the Vietnam War.

Baker observed male civil rights leaders of the SCLC, which SNCC had originally been a part of, express and act on their contempt for and prejudice against women. Male supremacy—the idea that women are controlled by and are less than men—dominated the SCLC.

When Baker became less involved in SNCC due to health reasons and men took over, it, too, was called out for sexism. Casey Hayden and Mary King, two female SNCC activists, wrote a memo to other female members in which they paralleled the treatment of African Americans in society to the treatment of women in SNCC. This memo became known as a **manifesto** for the feminist movement.

Black Women's Liberation

Through SNCC, the Black Women's Liberation Committee started in 1968 as a way of tackling SNCC's treatment of women as inferior. Fran Beal was one of the committee's founders. It was alarming, she said, when everyone was talking about liberation on the racial side, but then the men would turn around and talk about putting women in their place. In 1970, the group was renamed the Black Women's Alliance (BWA), becoming independent from SNCC but maintaining close political ties with it. Later that

A member of the Third World Women's Alliance at the Women's Strike for Equality in New York City.

A women's liberation group shows its support for the Black Panther Party in New Haven, Connecticut.

year, the group's common work with Puerto Rican women transformed the BWA into the Third World Women's Alliance (TWWA). The alliance distributed Beal's "Double Jeopardy: To Be Black and Female," a defining text on Black feminism that explored the different types of oppression Black women faced.

Unbought and Unbossed

Shirley Chisholm's memoir *Unbought and Unbossed*, published June 1, 1970, was a feminist piece detailing how she'd managed to be successful in politics despite being Black and a woman. She wrote that being a woman threw far more obstacles in her path. She was elected to Congress in 1968, becoming its first Black female member. She wrote the fact that she was a national figure only because she was a female Black member of Congress showed that America needed to see more Black women in politics.

Chisholm wrote that the prejudices against women were so widespread that they weren't even noticed—they were just accepted.

Chisholm aimed to change the way women were treated in America and, later that year, would team up with fellow representative Martha Griffiths to get things started. ■

The first black woman elected to Congress speaks out on her life and on the American political system

Shirley Chisholm wrote in her memoir that liberty and justice were only for white males.

U.S. Representative Martha Griffiths was determined to get the Equal Rights Amendment passed by Congress.

A large New Haven, Connecticut, crowd attends a rally supporting the jailed Black Panther Party leaders in May 1970.

4

Protests

Students had been upset with the war in Vietnam since its onset. Not only were they being drafted to shoot at people they had no conflict with and possibly be killed—they also felt that the war was unjustified and **unconstitutional**, as Congress had never formally declared war on Vietnam.

On April 30, when President Nixon announced that the conflict was growing to include an attack on Cambodia, America's students knew the time had come to act.

On May 1, at college and high school campuses across the country, students went on strike from their classes and held demonstrations to protest the expanded war. For the most part, these protests were disorganized and scattered. But things became organized fast, due to that day's massive strike in New Haven, Connecticut.

Tens of thousands of students, civil rights

activists, professors, Black Panther Party leaders, and community members gathered in the city's center, with an additional agenda: to free Bobby Seale and other Black Panthers being held in prison.

Seale had been moved from the prison in San Francisco to Connecticut to stand trial for the 1969 murder of a fellow Black Panther. These protesters felt that Seale was a political prisoner, charged not because he really committed a crime, but because he spoke out against the government.

The Murder of Alex Rackley

On May 17, 1969, members of the New Haven Black Panther Party kidnapped 19-year-old Alex Rackley, a fellow Panther who they suspected of being an FBI informant. After forcing a confession from him, they killed him. Rackley's body was found the next day, and several Panthers were arrested. Two of them admitted to their roles and agreed to testify against other defendants in exchange for lighter sentences. A third Panther, Lonnie McLucas, admitted his guilt but insisted on a trial. One of the two Panthers who took the agreement to testify claimed that Bobby Seale, who had been in New Haven hours before the murder, had ordered Rackley be killed. He also accused Ericka Huggins, founder of the New Haven Black Panthers chapter, of agreeing that Rackley should be killed. Seale and Huggins were charged with first-degree murder.

Nearly a year later, jury selection was about to begin for McLucas's trial.

A newspaper clipping of Black Panther member Lonnie McLucas during his trial for the murder of Alex Rackley (right).

Liberation News Service

UPI
McLucas (left), victim Rackley: The system was also in the dock

National Strike Information Center

The New Haven student protesters, who had traveled from all over the East Coast, felt so strongly about Seale and the Panthers that they formed the National Strike Information Center. They devised a phone system, headquartered at Brandeis University in Massachusetts, where strikes around the country could report in as part of the mass protest, and they also started a newsletter. Inside this newsletter they listed three demands for ending the nationwide strikes.

First, they demanded that "the U.S. government end its repression of political protest and release all political prisoners, such as Bobby Seale and other members of the Black Panther Party." The second demand was that the United States

The National Strike Information Center newsletter helped organize student strikes all over the country.

withdraw troops from Vietnam and Cambodia. The third was that universities stop aiding the government to recruit students for war through providing research and allowing armed forces recruitment on their campuses.

New Haven's Yale University students were a large part of this protest, sharing their dormitory rooms with protesters from out of town. But even Yale president Kingman Brewster, Jr., issued a public statement in support of the Panthers, saying that he doubted a Black revolutionary could receive a fair trial anywhere in the United States.

The FBI's abuse of authority and persecution of people and groups they perceived as threats was well-known, as was Nixon's embracing of these tactics. The treatment of the defendants in Chicago—and especially the treatment Seale received—showed that the court system was equally capable of violating civil rights.

The phone banks were set up by that night—and the calls began coming in. The student strike was more than just individual demonstrations on campuses—it was a nationwide statement that students were not going to just sit by. It was something big.

Kent State

Most of the protests were peaceful. At Kent State University in Ohio, students began protesting on Friday, May 1. The protesters planned for a larger rally on Monday, May 4, at noon. The National Guard had been called in over the weekend to break up any demonstrations. Due to the rising tensions between the protesters and guards, university officials tried to ban the rally on Monday morning. But most of the students were unaware of this ban, and many showed up to continue protesting.

No one was ever arrested or held accountable for the Kent State shootings on May 4, 1970.

Midday, unarmed students found themselves facing a barricade of National Guardsmen. A group of these guardsmen huddled together, and they opened fire on the students for 13 seconds—killing four students.

These senseless killings escalated the protests around the country. No explanation for the tragic shootings was offered, and no guardsmen were charged with a crime.

Jackson State

On the evening of May 14, about 100 Black students at Jackson State College (now Jackson State University) in Jackson, Mississippi, were gathered at the edge of the campus on Lynch Street, a main road. They were concerned about racism, something they faced daily in Jackson once they left the campus. In fact, Lynch Street was a place where they would meet insults from white motorists. They were especially upset because of a false rumor about the death of Charles Evers, a civil rights activist. As the evening went on, they reportedly threw rocks at white motorists. The fire department arrived to put out the fires and requested police assistance.

By midnight, the students had ceased their behavior, and some had left. The police moved in to disperse the remaining students who were in front of Alexander Hall, a dormitory.

Music as Protest

The chaos of the world was reflected in two hit 1970 songs by African American artists, both released on Motown Records. The band the Temptations' "Ball of Confusion (That's What the World Is Today)" reached number three on the pop charts and number two on the R&B charts.

Edwin Starr's "War" is a powerful song protesting the Vietnam War. Originally recorded by the Temptations, Starr's recording of the song rose to the number-one spot on the R&B charts for three weeks in 1970. He also won a Grammy Award for Best Male R&B Vocal Performance.

As time went on, the song's message continued to resonate as a cry to end all war, and performers such as Frankie Goes to Hollywood and Bruce Springsteen sang versions of it.

Edwin Starr's "War" sold over 3 million copies.

The students were not engaging in any threatening behavior and did nothing to antagonize the police.

At 12:05 a.m., the police opened fire on the students. Forty highway patrolmen fired over 460 shotgun blasts for 28 seconds. When it was over, two young men were dead: Phillip Lafayette Gibbs, a 21-year-old pre-law junior with a wife, child, and a baby on the way, and James Earl Green, a 17-year-old Jim Hill High School senior who had stopped to see what was going on as he walked home from his job at the supermarket.

The police said that they had fired in response to a shooting from the roof. No evidence of a shooter was ever found.

Phillip Lafayette Gibbs.

James Earl Green.

Breaking the Race Barrier

Kenneth A. Gibson was a Black structural engineer from Newark, New Jersey. In June, he defeated the two-term sitting mayor of Newark to become the city's first African American mayor—and the first

Mayor Kenneth A. Gibson (seated) wanted Newark's businesses to pay more taxes and help improve the community.

KENNETH A. GIBSON
MAYOR

African American mayor of a major Northeastern city.

Gibson had big plans for Newark. He wanted to attract major industry to provide jobs. The election was a bitter fight. Hugh J. Addonizio, the current mayor, was on trial for criminal charges during the last weeks of the campaign. He was later convicted.

Gibson's candidacy attracted nationwide attention. He opened seven community health centers, improved Newark's budget, and instituted a plan that ended discrimination in government hiring. Gibson also established street repaving programs and reduced the city's crime rate by 25 percent.

Octavia Spencer

Octavia Spencer was born on May 25, 1970, in Montgomery, Alabama. She is one of two Black actresses to receive three Academy Award nominations, and the first to be nominated two years in a row.

Spencer's first role was in the 1996 film *A Time to Kill*. She had many roles in film, TV, and theater in the following years. Her breakout role was in 2011's *The Help*, for which she won the Academy Award for Best Supporting Actress for playing Minny Jackson, an assured, spunky maid.

Spencer was nominated again for her role in 2016's *Hidden Figures*, portraying one of the real-life Black women mathematicians who were critical to NASA's space program in the 1960s. The following year, she was nominated for her role as a cleaning woman in 2017's *The Shape of Water*. Spencer became the first Black woman to receive back-to-back nominations.

Octavia Spencer (center) portrays mathematician Dorothy Vaughn in the film *Hidden Figures*.

Essence Magazine

The first issue of *Essence* magazine was published in May 1970. Written for African American women, the magazine focuses on culture, entertainment, beauty, and fashion. It has included articles on controversial topics as well, such as Black politics and the criminal justice system. Distinguished African American writers Maya Angelou, Amiri Baraka, and Nikki Giovanni have had original work featured in *Essence*.

ESSENCE

SENSUAL
BLACK
MAN,
DO
YOU
LOVE ME?

PLAYTIME
VINES

DYNAMITE
AFROS

REVOLT:
FROM
ROSA
TO
KATHLEEN

CAREERS:
DATA
PROCESSING

The premier issue of *Essence* magazine featured model Barbara Cheeseborough.

A New Tactic

On June 11, U.S. Representative Martha Griffiths from Michigan filed a petition to vote on the proposed Equal Rights Amendment.

Griffiths had been a member of Congress since 1955. Every year, she had introduced this resolution at the start of Congress's session. And every year, she watched as the Judiciary Committee refused to send it out to be considered by the full House of Representatives.

After 15 years of frustration, Griffiths was determined to succeed. ▪

Martha Griffiths was the first Michigan woman elected to Congress from the Democratic Party.

A New Jersey state policeman beats a man who refuses to move from the train tracks during the Asbury Park Uprising.

5

Race Riots

An unemployment crisis triggered the Asbury Park Uprising, which occurred between July 4 and July 10. Asbury Park, New Jersey, was a seaside town that attracted many tourists during the warmer months. Black youth who lived permanently in the city relied on employment from tourism. But increasingly, white youth from neighboring communities were given these jobs. Poor housing conditions and a lack of parks, playing fields, and basketball courts to engage in added to the spark that ignited this major civil disturbance.

Seven days of turmoil began by Black youth breaking windows of local businesses following a dance they had attended. This quickly escalated to looting and firebombs.

Within days, more than 180 people, including 15 New Jersey state troopers, were injured.

Forty-six people were sent to the hospital with gunshot wounds. The state police were at a loss as to why so many people had been shot. They said their officers had fired warning shots in the air.

Asbury Park's largely Black West Side neighborhood was destroyed. The shopping and business section was especially hit hard. The cost of the damage was estimated at $5,600,000.

On July 8, Asbury Park officials, representatives of the governor, and local Black leaders met to try to reach a solution to end the riots. African American representatives had sent a list of 20 demands, including the appointment of Black citizens on the board of education and the creation of jobs for Black youth.

In the devastated community, "Citizen Peace Patrols" walked the streets, urging people to be peaceful and obey the curfew that had been established. The National Guard also arrived to establish order.

The rioting ended on July 10. President Nixon was asked to declare the West Side a major disaster area so it could receive **federal** funds to help rebuild, but he did not.

ERA Unleashed

On July 20, Martha Griffiths achieved what many people thought was impossible. She secured 218 signatures from members of Congress on her petition to release and vote for the Equal Rights Amendment. She had worked tirelessly, approaching members in their offices and discussing what the document meant and why they should sign it. Sometimes their reluctance was not a personal stance against equal rights, but concern over how to explain it to the voters that they represented. Griffiths took the time to help them see how they could do that.

On August 10, Griffiths brought the ERA to the House floor for discussion and a vote. Shirley Chisholm then delivered a powerful speech endorsing the proposed amendment. She said that prejudice against African Americans was starting to become unacceptable in America because white people were beginning to admit that it existed. But prejudice against women was still acceptable, with few people seeing the "immorality" in smaller pay scales for women and most of the better jobs available for men only.

Six of the 12 female members of the U.S. House of Representatives sit in the office of the Speaker of the House.

"Women do not have the opportunities that men do," Chisholm stated. She added that women who did not conform to the system and tried to break the pattern were labeled "odd" and "unfeminine." She said it was time to begin the process of change.

The members of the House of Representatives passed the motion for the ERA to be added to the Constitution. It went on to the Senate.

Women Strike

The National Organization for Women organized the Women's Strike for Equality on August 26—50 years after women gained the right to vote in America. It was phenomenally successful, with about 50,000 women gathering in New York City and even more across the country.

The women's liberation movement struggled with gaining large-scale support from Black women, however.

During the Strike for Equality, women march down New York's Madison Avenue.

The Mangrove Nine

The Mangrove in London, England, was a Caribbean restaurant where the Notting Hill neighborhood's Black community gathered, including Black intellectuals and activists. The restaurant was repeatedly raided by the police, who suspected drug possession inside—even though there was never any evidence produced.

On August 9, 1970, 150 Black Power activists marched to the police station to protest the obviously racial targeting of The Mangrove. Seven men and two women were arrested after violence broke out between protesters and police. The protesters were charged with starting a riot.

Two of the Mangrove Nine decided to defend themselves in court. The defendants were all cleared of the rioting charges, but four of them received sentences for lesser charges. This was the first time a judge had acknowledged racial prejudice by London's Metropolitan Police. It inspired other civil rights activists to challenge authorities.

The *Women's Rights Law Reporter*

In the summer of 1970, Ann Marie Boylan, a recent Rutgers Law School graduate, published the first volume of the *Women's Rights Law Reporter* out of her New York City apartment. A legal journal focused on women's rights was unheard of, and she could not raise support for it. She did not know if she could afford to continue the publication.

Boylan was part of a women's group made up of recent law school graduates who gathered to support one another in a male-dominated profession. Elizabeth Langer, another member, decided to approach the dean at Rutgers University in New Jersey about publishing it through the school. The dean agreed with conditions, one of which was that Rutgers would fund the journal. He also insisted they find a faculty adviser and an advisory board.

Professor Ruth Bader Ginsburg happily agreed to be their staff adviser. Ginsburg would later become the second woman to serve on the U.S. Supreme Court. Langer found three advisory board members, including Eleanor Holmes Norton.

After meeting the dean's conditions, the *Reporter* belonged to Rutgers. Today it remains the oldest American legal journal focusing on women's rights law.

Ruth Bader Ginsburg was the first female to be appointed a full professor at Columbia Law School.

Signs read: "I'M NO BREEDER FOR THE MAN'S WAR", "SISTERHOOD IS POWERFUL— END THE WAR!", "THE WOMEN OF VIETNAM ARE OUR SISTERS"

The August Women's Strike included a cry for peace in Vietnam.

Many African American women felt that their issues were different than those of white women, and they did not think that white women would work adequately to secure the rights Black women needed.

Black women distrusted the women's liberation movement because of the long history of white people using and abusing African Americans. They were not convinced that the women's movement served in their best interest. They doubted that the movement understood the distinctiveness of their own Black experiences.

But there were some African American women in attendance at the strike. Eleanor Holmes Norton was one of them. The ACLU attorney had recently become the head of New York City's Commission on Human Rights. She was there in the center of the crowd, wearing a traditional African outfit, trying her best to show Black women it was the right thing to join the movement. ■

ACLU attorney Eleanor Holmes Norton (center) conducts a press conference during the discrimination lawsuit against *Newsweek* magazine.

6

Searching for Fairness

On the same day as the Women's Strike for Equality, Eleanor Holmes Norton celebrated a legal victory for women's rights. As an attorney for the ACLU, she represented 60 female employees of *Newsweek*, a major weekly news magazine. The women filed a claim with the Equal Employment Opportunity Commission (EEOC), a federal agency that enforces civil rights laws against discrimination in the workplace. The claim stated that *Newsweek*'s employment policy was discriminatory against women, who were never allowed an opportunity to be reporters, writers, and editors. Women at the magazine were researchers for stories, which was the lowest-paying and least-acknowledged job.

Norton won the discrimination case for the women, and on August 26, she signed an agreement with *Newsweek*'s editor in chief on the women's behalf. This agreement stated that *Newsweek* would take specific steps to hire women for the higher positions, and this would be accomplished within a year.

Massive Demonstration

The National **Chicano** Moratorium Committee Against the Vietnam War, often called the Chicano Moratorium, was a coalition of Mexican American groups who came together to demand an end to the

Mexican American demonstrators at the August Chicano Moratorium march.

Vietnam War. The committee organized a march that occurred on August 29, attracting 30,000 demonstrators—one of the biggest gatherings of Mexican Americans ever. This demonstration was the largest anti-war action carried out by an American **ethnic** group.

A Fair Trial

In September, the first New Haven Panther trial ended after 11 weeks. Lonnie McLucas had confessed to murdering Alex Rackley, but he had refused to accept a plea bargain, which meant his case would be tried in court. This court case tested whether a Black revolutionary could receive a fair trial in the United States. It was a capital case, meaning that the defendant could receive the death penalty if convicted.

The jury selection had taken six weeks and resulted in a jury made up mainly of white jurors. Protesters were concerned that McLucas would be immediately convicted by a racist jury—but this did not happen.

After deliberating for six days, the jury cleared McLucas of the capital murder charge. Instead, he was convicted of conspiracy to commit murder, receiving a 12-to-15-year prison sentence. His lawyer stated that the judge was fair, the jury was fair, and, in this case, a Black revolutionary had received a fair trial in the United States.

Dismissed

In October, Bobby Seale and Ericka Huggins went on trial for the Rackley murder. The jury selection took four months. Once again, the jury was made up mainly of white jurors.

The trial stretched on for six months. The case against Bobby Seale rested solely on the testimony of one man who claimed Seale had ordered the killing of Rackley. Huggins was charged because her voice was on the recording of Rackley's interrogation before he was murdered. Huggins claimed she had questioned Rackley under duress, meaning that she feared for her life if she didn't go along with what was happening.

On May 24, 1971, the jury announced that it could not reach a unanimous verdict for either defendant. They were deadlocked 11 to 1 for Seale's acquittal and 10 to 2 for Huggins's acquittal.

The next day, Judge Harold Mulvey delivered the shocking decision that he was dismissing the case against Seale and Huggins rather than retry them. He said that it was impossible to find an unbiased jury "without superhuman efforts."

Swann v. Charlotte-Mecklenburg Board of Education

The Supreme Court heard arguments in *Swann v. Charlotte-Mecklenburg Board of Education* on October 12, 1970. This landmark case had been brought by the NAACP Legal Defense Fund on behalf of nine African American children, including six-year-old James Swann, because their local schools were still not integrated 16 years after *Brown v. Board of Education* outlawed segregated schools.

North Carolina had accepted integration after the decision, but in Charlotte, students were enrolled in the schools closest to their homes. Black families and white families lived in separate neighborhoods far from one another so their schools were not integrated. The lawsuit was filed to force Charlotte to bus children to other schools so that schools would have an equal distribution of Black and white students.

The members of the Supreme Court were unhappy that their order to segregate schools had still not been carried out in many places. They realized that busing students was needed to integrate, and they unanimously voted in favor of Swann.

Black students in Charlotte-Mecklenburg attended schools that were either all Black or over 99 percent Black.

NORTH CAROLI   IC SCHOOLS
MECKLEN

ERA Blocked

In the fall, the ERA hit a roadblock in the Senate, which voted to amend it with a requirement excusing women from a military draft. This caused an uproar in Congress over whether women should carry the burdens as well as the privileges of equality. With tempers flaring and heated opinions flying, there was no way an agreement could be reached before the end of the congressional session. Griffiths vowed to undertake the process again in the next session.

Women make their desire for equality clear at a New York City rally supporting the ERA.

Free Angela

On October 13, 1970, a Black woman named Angela
Davis was arrested for the kidnapping and first-
degree murder of Judge Harold Haley.

Haley had been abducted as a hostage when
a trial he was presiding over was hijacked by a
gunman. Haley was killed while the gunman tried to
escape.

Angela Davis was not at the scene of the murder.
But she knew the gunman, and she owned the gun
that was used to commit the crime. She insisted
she was innocent but fled from the police before
they could arrest her. Davis feared she would not be
treated fairly.

Willis Reed

Willis Reed of the New York Knicks became the first African American basketball player to win the National Basketball Association's All-Star MVP, NBA Finals MVP, and NBA MVP all in the same season. Also in 1970, Reed was chosen as ABC's Wide World of Sports Athlete of the Year and the Sporting News NBA MVP. He was also chosen for the 1970 All-NBA First Team and the 1970 NBA All-Defensive First Team.

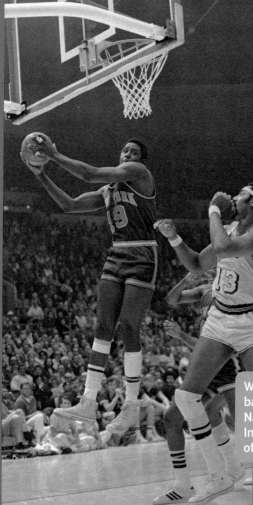

In Game Seven of the 1970 NBA Finals, Reed showed up to play despite a severe thigh injury, scoring the Knicks' first two field goals on his first two shot attempts. Famed sports commentator Howard Cosell told Reed afterward, "You exemplify the very best that the human spirit can offer."

Willis Reed (pictured with ball) was inducted into the National Association of Intercollegiate Athletics Hall of Fame in 1970.

The Third World Women's Alliance march in support of Angela Davis.

After nearly two months, Davis was found in New York City and arrested. Still maintaining her innocence, she was put in prison to await trial.

Her arrest and imprisonment became the subject of mass protests across the country.

Thousands of supporters across America organized a "Free Angela" movement.

As 1970 ended, the outcry over Angela Davis's incarceration grew. Black writers in New York City formed a group called Black People in Defense of Angela Davis.

Music was written about the injustice being done to her to raise money for her defense. One song was "Angela," by John Lennon and Yoko Ono. "Free Angela" became a battle cry for activists seeking fairness in an unjust land.

Members of New Haven's Black Panther Party await the outcome of Bobby Seale's trial.

The Legacy of 1970 in Civil Rights History

The year 1970 saw the inexcusable, shocking behavior of people in positions of authority, from the president of the United States, to the FBI, judges, the National Guard, and the police. Leaders of a democracy are supposed to protect the rights and the lives of its citizens, but in many instances, they did the opposite.

President Richard Nixon seemingly thought nothing of sending thousands of young men to fight and possibly die in Vietnam. It appeared he also thought nothing of letting the FBI falsely accuse and charge citizens who he perceived as threats to national security.

On May 13, 1971, after an eight-month trial, the Panther 21 defendants were acquitted of all charges. It was discovered that undercover FBI informants had infiltrated the Black Panther Party, and that they were the ones who suggested the bomb plots.

It was also revealed that the FBI had sent undercover agents to pose as protesters who picketed outside the Bernsteins' apartment building after the Panther 21 fundraiser. The agents were sent to create negative public opinion of the Bernsteins.

Nixon established the President's Commission on Campus Unrest to investigate both the Jackson State and Kent State tragedies, but no arrests were ever made—and no reasons were ever offered for either of the shootings.

At the end of 1970, the "Free Angela" movement immediately sprang into action—perhaps

William Scranton concluded in his report that the Kent State shootings were unjustified.

THE PRESIDENT'S COMMISSION ON CAMPUS UNREST

The Black Panthers join with the Young Lords in Chicago, Illinois, protesting the trial of Bobby Seale in April 1970.

accelerated by all the previous injustices that had occurred against vulnerable and discriminated-against citizens. This movement would push through 1971 and into 1972, when Davis finally got her day in court and received her freedom. ■

Aileen Hernandez

Aileen Hernandez was a Black woman with a passion for both civil rights and women's rights. The first woman to serve on the federal government's Equal Employment Opportunity Commission, Hernandez targeted discrimination against job applicants based on race or gender. As president of the National Organization for Women, she sought to increase the membership of Black women. Throughout her life, Hernandez set her sights on ending all discrimination, saying she could not close her eyes to the mistreatment of any group.

Aileen Hernandez testifies before a Congressional committee in support of the Equal Rights Amendment.

Born in Brooklyn, New York, on May 23, 1926, Aileen was the only daughter of Jamaican immigrants. Charles Henry Clarke, Sr., a brush salesman, and Ethel Louise Hall, a seamstress, raised their three children in Bay Ridge, an all-white neighborhood. Aileen learned about discrimination at an early age when a neighbor started a petition to force the Clarkes out of their home. Ethel took five-year-old Aileen by the hand and headed over to that neighbor's house, giving him a lecture about their family and why they were there. When she finished, she simply turned and walked out. This was Aileen's

Hernandez was dedicated to helping economically challenged women.

first exposure to activism, and even though she was young, she learned a lot that day.

Activism drifted to the back of her mind as she grew up. She moved to Washington, DC, by train to study education at Howard University, a historically Black college. At the DC station, she asked someone how to get to the Howard campus. He told her to take a "black" cab. Thinking he meant she should find a taxi that was painted black, she soon realized the ugly truth: The man had been referring to the color of

"The Black struggle and our struggle are the same revolution—the human revolution."

—AILEEN HERNANDEZ

Hernandez championed all minorities and made sure they were not denied jobs based on their race or gender.

the driver's skin. This experience made activism become more important to Hernandez than anything else. She changed her academic focus to sociology and political science and joined the campus chapter of the NAACP.

Graduating with honors in 1947, Hernandez became an international exchange student and studied at the University of Oslo in Norway. When she returned to America, she spotted an opportunity to become a labor leader for the International Ladies Garment Workers Union (ILGWU). She headed to California for a year of training and then went to work as a union organizer for the ILGWU, which protected female factory workers' rights. In her 10 years working for the ILGWU, Hernandez rose to become the education and public relations director of the union's West Coast division.

In 1965, President Lyndon B. Johnson appointed Hernandez to the newly formed EEOC,

Hernandez was given the civil liberties award by the Northern California chapter of the ACLU for "decades of work for equality and justice."

which would enforce the new workplace anti-discrimination laws that were part of the Civil Rights Act of 1964. Hernandez was the only woman serving on the five-member commission. She became frustrated when the commission avoided acting in cases involving gender discrimination. She told the other members that the commission had no right to pick and choose which kind of discrimination they would attack. She left the commission in 1966, becoming a founder of NOW and their executive vice president.

In 1970, Hernandez became the second president of NOW. She urged Black women to join the organization, saying that the women's struggle and the Black struggle were the same revolution—the human revolution.

Testifying at a Senate hearing to urge passage of the Equal Rights Amendment, Hernandez stated that women were outraged by the discrimination they received in America, and they were determined to become first-class citizens. She also oversaw the Women's Strike for Equality marches in August 1970, which celebrated the 50th anniversary of women earning the right to vote as well as the new feminist movement in which women across the country were demanding equal rights with men.

The following year, Hernandez chaired a committee that sparked the National Women's Political Caucus. This group was dedicated to gaining political power

for women. Shirley Chisholm was one of the group's leaders. Hernandez had a style that was both warm and authoritative, which made her excellent at organizing people to work together.

Continuing her dedication to fight the double discrimination Black women faced, Hernandez was a founder of the groups Black Women Stirring the Waters and Black Women Organized for Political Action. She also ran a consulting firm that challenged gender and racial discrimination.

Hernandez believed that Black women were like no other women in the world, having managed to survive in a world in which both racism and sexism were everywhere. She was proud of her accomplishments and happy to see the progress toward civil and women's rights in her lifetime, but she stressed that the work for equality was far from done. Young people were the ones who could finish that work. ∎

Hernandez (third from left) appears in the 2013 PBS documentary *Makers: Women Who Make America*.

TIMELINE

The Year in Civil Rights

1970

APRIL 30

President Nixon announces that the conflict in Vietnam is growing to include an attack on Cambodia.

MAY 4

Four students are killed by National Guardsmen at a protest at Kent State University in Ohio.

JANUARY 14

Conductor Leonard Bernstein and his wife, Felicia Montealegre, host a controversial fundraiser for the Panther 21.

MAY 2

The Jackson 5 holds their first concert as Motown artists at the Philadelphia Civic Center.

FEBRUARY 14

The trial of the Chicago Seven goes to the jury for deliberations.

JUNE 1

Shirley Chisholm's memoir *Unbought and Unbossed* is published.

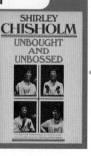

JULY 4

The Asbury Park Uprising begins in New Jersey.

AUGUST 29

The National Chicano Moratorium Committee organizes 30,000 protesters against the Vietnam War.

JULY 17

The second Black Panther liberation school opens in Mount Vernon, New York.

OCTOBER 12

The Supreme Court hears arguments in the *Swann v. Charlotte-Mecklenburg Board of Education* case.

AUGUST 26

The National Organization for Women march in the Women's Strike for Equality in New York City.

OCTOBER 13

Angela Davis is arrested for the kidnapping and first-degree murder of Judge Harold Haley.

GLOSSARY

abolish (uh-BAH-lish) to put an end to something officially

acquit (uh-KWIT) to find someone not guilty of a crime

activist (AK-tuh-vist) a person who works to bring about political or social change

amendment (uh-MEND-muhnt) a change that is made to a law or a legal document

boycott (BOI-kaht) a refusal to buy something or do business with someone as a protest

Chicano (chi-KAH-noh) an American, especially a man or boy, of Mexican descent

civil rights (SIV-uhl rites) the individual rights that all members of a democratic society have to freedom and equal treatment under the law

conspiracy (kuhn-SPEER-uh-see) a secret plan made by two or more people to do something illegal or harmful

contempt (kuhn-TEMPT) the belief that something is worthless and deserves no respect

defendant (di-FEN-duhnt) the person in a court case who has been accused of a crime or who is being sued

deliberation (di-lib-uh-RAY-shuhn) the act of considering something carefully

desegregation (dee-seg-ruh-GAY-shuhn) the practice of doing away with separating people of different races in schools, restaurants, and other public places

discrimination (dis-krim-uh-NAY-shuhn) prejudice or unfair behavior to others based on differences in such things as race, gender, or age

draft a system in which young people are required to join the armed forces of a country for a period of service

economic (ek-uh-NAH-mik) of or having to do with the way money, resources, and services are used in a society

ethnic (ETH-nik) of or having to do with a group of people sharing the same national origins, language, or culture

exploitation (ek-sploi-TAY-shuhn) the practice of treating someone unfairly for your own advantage

federal (FED-ur-uhl) having to do with the national government, as opposed to state or local government

feminist (FEM-uh-nist) someone who believes strongly that women are equal to men and should have the same rights and opportunities

integration (in-ti-GRAY-shuhn) the act or practice of making facilities or an organization open to people of all races and ethnic groups

Jim Crow (jim kro) the former practice of segregating Black people in the United States

liberation (lib-uh-RAY-shuhn) the act of freeing someone or something from imprisonment, slavery, or oppression

lynching (LIN-ching) a sometimes public murder by a group of people, often involving hanging

manifesto (man-uh-FES-toh) a written statement that describes the policies, goals, and opinions of a person or group

Nation of Islam (NAY-shuhn uhv IZ-lahm) an African American movement and organization that combines the religion of Islam with Black Nationalist ideas

nonviolent resistance (nahn-VYE-uh-luhnt ri-ZIS-tuhns) peaceful demonstration for political purpose

racist (RAY-sist) someone who thinks that a particular race is better than others or treats people unfairly or cruelly because of their race

segregation (seg-ruh-GAY-shuhn) the act or practice of keeping people or groups apart

suffrage (SUHF-rij) the right to vote

unconstitutional (uhn-kahn-sti-TOO-shuh-uhl) not in keeping with the basic principles or laws set forth in the U.S. Constitution

white supremacist (wite suh-PRE-muh-sist) a person with the belief that white people are superior to people of color and that white people should have control over those who they do not view as white

91

BIBLIOGRAPHY

Aronson, Marc. *Master of Deceit: J. Edgar Hoover and America in the Age of Lies.* Somerville, MA: Candlewick Press, 2012.

Cone, James H. *Martin & Malcolm & America: A Dream or a Nightmare.* 20th anniversary ed. Maryknoll, NY: Orbis, 2012.

Davis, Angela Y., ed. *If They Come in the Morning: Voices of Resistance.* New York: Penguin, 1972.

Dore, Mary, dir. *She's Beautiful When She's Angry.* 2014.

Levine, Mark L., George C. McNamee, and Daniel L. Greenberg, eds. *The Trial of the Chicago Seven*: The Official Transcript. New York: Simon & Schuster, 2020.

Shames, Stephen, and Bobby Seale. *Power to the People: The World of the Black Panthers.* New York: Abrams, 2016.

Newly elected congresswoman Shirley Chisholm on the Capitol steps before delivering a speech to the House of Representatives.

INDEX

About the Author

Selene Castrovilla is an acclaimed, award-winning author. Her five books on the American Revolution for young readers include Scholastic's *The Founding Mothers*. Selene has been a meticulous researcher of American history since 2003. She has expanded her exploration into the civil rights movement, as well as the Civil War, in a forthcoming book. A frequent speaker about our nation's evolution, she is equally comfortable with audiences of children and adults. Please visit selenecastrovilla.com.

PHOTO CREDITS